Embracing Disability in Early Childhood

Supporting Children Living with a Disability and their Families in Early Childhood Settings.

Jenny Nechvatal

Bachelor of Education

(Early Childhood Education)

Embracing Disability in Early Childhood

Copyright © 2024 Jenny Nechvatal

All rights reserved.

ISBN: 978-0-646-89627-4

ACKNOWLEDGEMENTS

This book is dedicated to Ryan and Zac Nechvatal.

To my husband Tony Nechvatal, thank you for sharing this parenting journey with me. It has been very different to what we expected, your determination that Ryan and Zac receive the best services, education and opportunities has had a positive impact on their life. Our family will always be grateful to you for this passion and purpose.

To my daughter Kate Nechvatal, we couldn't be prouder of the amazing adult you have become. Your support and love for Ryan and Zac is such a gift to them, the way their faces light up when they see you, I know that love is returned. We know their future is secure with you as their champion and advocate. Thank you for your input into the editing and design of this book.

To Colleen Murphy, Cassy Read, Tash Mannion and Tracy Wales, thank you for your editing skills and early childhood knowledge, your input has been invaluable. Ailish Keating for your cheerleading role through all the processes of writing this book.

To the dedicated Educators at Amy Hurd Early Learning Centre thank you for being a sounding board at the start of the writing process, your input helped to define the content.

Lisa Eastley, Kylie Doolan and Cathy Manning thank you for sharing your diagnosis stories in such an honest, open and heartwarming manner.

CONTENTS

	Introduction	i
1	Reality of Receiving a Diagnosis	1
2	Stages of Diagnosis	6
3	Accessing an Early Childhood Service	15
4	Supporting Children in Your Service	18
5	Hard Conversations, Strategies and Techniques to Support Families	29
6	Supporting Yourself and Your Team	39
7	Parent Reaction and Parent Stories	43
8	Early Intervention, Supports and Pedagogy	48
9	Siblings their Role and the Support They Need	61
	Resources and Further Info	63

INTRODUCTION

When I started my teaching career, I wasn't confident teaching children with a disability. This was because of my lack of awareness and understanding of disability. When I was growing up, disability was hidden in the community. I didn't have any friends or family members with a disability. I wasn't familiar or comfortable with people who had a disability.

As a result of my limited experience and awareness, I lacked the necessary skills to confidently interact with people living with a disability. I found it difficult to be positive when teaching children living with a disability in the early childhood setting. As my career progressed, the inclusion and acceptance of those living with disabilities in early childhood services and the broader community increased. I developed a better understanding of how to engage and teach children with a disability.

However, it wasn't until I had my children with a disability that I finally understood; that it all 'clicked'. My children opened my eyes to supporting other children living with a disability. Managing the emotional highs and lows, I learned to adjust learning activities to meet children's specific needs, and authentically include them in the service environment. It also allowed me to deeply understand the family's perspective and the difficulties many families face. I had now personally lived the experience of the diagnosis process and the wide range of complicated feelings that come with it. I understood the impact this experience had on myself and my family, which I have since learned is a very common one.

Now I want to share my knowledge and experience with early childhood educators to help them be more inclusive to children and families with a disability. My combined professional and lived experience can provide educators with the knowledge and insight required to provide supportive and inclusive environments for children with a disability.

Early childhood education is an area that I have been passionate about for many years. I strongly believe in the benefits of early childhood education for all children. The importance of early childhood intervention for all children with a disability is well documented. Research shows that when children attend a supportive and inclusive early childhood service the opportunities for them to learn and develop increase. When working alongside families and early intervention providers early childhood educators can and do have a significant positive impact on a child's development. Unfortunately, for educators who are not confident or who lack this knowledge, the opposite is true for these children.

I have worked in the early childhood sector for 33 years holding the positions of Teacher, Director, and Head of Department at TAFE. I currently run a support coordination business for NDIS participants, connecting them to the services they require in their local community. I write about the reality of raising children with a disability and consult with early childhood services.

As you read this book you will learn

Stages of diagnosis

The reality of receiving a diagnosis

How to support families at the time of and after a diagnosis

Parents' concerns over their child attending an early childhood service.

Practical suggestions for conversations with families

Understanding types of therapies

Why therapy is so important and the early childhood educators' role.

Definitions and Terminology:

Educator: the term educator refers to all trained professionals in the role of Certificate III, Diploma and Bachelor of Early Childhood.

NDIS: The National Disability Insurance Scheme. A government organisation that funds people with a disability to access the services and supports they require to achieve their highest level of independence while engaging with services and within their community.

Neurodiversity: the diversity of the human mind. It describes the range of differences in individual brain functioning and behaviour, regarded as part of the variance in human populations. Reference: (Australian Government Department of Education, 2022)

1 REALITY OF RECEIVING A DIAGNOSIS

The impacts on individuals and their families:

We all experience moments that can change our lives forever. Our moment was eighteen years ago when our pediatrician said "Jenny, Tony. Your boys are autistic". A very blunt statement with no room for argument, there was no attempt to soften the words that would change the future of our boys and our family forever. From that day, our family's life changed. Along with our preconceived ideas of family life, and the hopes and dreams we had for our family. We had to develop a new way of understanding our children, adapting to, and accommodating to meet their needs within a society that didn't always recognise their needs.

Immediately after the diagnosis, there were a range of emotions, sadness, anger, worry, confusion, and frustration. Despite these mixed emotions, the constant underlying emotion was love, because you love your children no matter what. As parents, we became very fearful of what their life would be like. How the community would or would not accept them. It became a priority to support and advocate for them. Being an advocate for our sons has remained constant as they have moved through life. As children go through their stages of life, parents will be required to adjust, decide, implement, and meet the everyday needs of their children constantly.

As an early childhood educator, you work with families who don't want to recognise or admit that their child has a disability. Parents can remain in this stage for varying periods of time. Some will move through it fluidly, whereas others may remain rigid in this mindset for extended periods. Before the diagnosis, I took on the role of denial. Despite the gentle suggestions from family and friends saying we should get my son's speech and hearing checked. Another example of my denial was when my sons would toe walk. People regularly commented on this. I can remember saying "The only children I know who walk on their tiptoes are Autistic, but my sons aren't Autistic". Yes, alarm bells were ringing but I didn't want to hear them.

Despite my background in early childhood, I was rigid in my denial, especially compared to my husband. My education and training underpinned by knowledge of child development, caused an internal battle between my heart and my brain. Knowing there was likely something wrong but wishing for them to lead the lives we had imagined for them. Once we received the official diagnosis, I still didn't want to accept the reality. When it is a personal experience, all training, knowledge, and common sense go out the window. You don't want to acknowledge there is something wrong with your precious child or children.

Denial ensured I avoided acknowledging the truth for some time. It was a difficult stage I had to go through as a parent. I can remember telling the President of the management committee at the early childhood centre where I worked about my son's diagnosis. Her response was "I'm sorry Jenny. We never want anything to be wrong with our children". The stigma and pain of a diagnosis means there is something wrong with your child. This is the driving force for the denial that parents experience. As a result, it is common for parents to deny their child's developmental delays or disabilities for as long as they can, and some will never acknowledge it.

The denial presented by parents can be difficult to manage from an educator's perspective. You are in this role as a trained professional to support all children and see them thrive and develop. When parents accept their child's diagnosis or developmental delay. Parents and educators can work together proactively creating a supportive team around the child. This state of denial can vary in length depending on the individual parents' journey. You may find in some family dynamics, that one parent remains in denial, whilst the other progresses forward. The parents' stage of denial will likely be because of the concerns and fears they are processing regarding their child's development. What does their progression to school and further into adult life look like? It is normal for educators to also have these concerns regarding development and the child's livelihood once they progress onwards from your service. To support families and educators regarding these common concerns and stressors many communities offer early intervention programs.

Early Intervention programs are designed for children aged 0-7 years, aiming to support the development of skills for school readiness and adult life. These programs also provide support and education to families on supporting their children. With the additional benefit of connecting them with other individuals experiencing similar emotions and challenges. As educators, it can be challenging to support children when parents are hesitant or resistant to engage in early intervention programs. I will discuss this and possible solutions in more detail in Chapter 6 – Supporting Yourself and Your Team.

After the diagnosis, parenting took on a whole new look. There were numerous new worries and issues to deal with that we had not expected as parents. At the time of diagnosis, we had many fears and concerns. Our concerns included our children's wellbeing. Would others accept them? What would their and our future look like as a family?

The biggest question for us was "How do you raise two children with a disability?"

This was uncharted territory for us, despite my background in early childhood. I knew how to educate. I didn't know how to manage the day-to-day changes that would come our way. At the time of diagnosis, we knew very little about this disability, nor where we could go to learn what we needed to know. We were in a constant spiral of questions and worry. How would this affect our children, our family, and our future?

Disability is now much more accepted, normalised, and understood within society. However, eighteen years ago when our boys were diagnosed the broader community was not accepting and there were still significantly negative perceptions of disability. This was extremely daunting as a parent when we received our boy's diagnosis. We had very few positive experiences to gauge what our experience would be. We had significant concerns about their future and how their life would look. It has been amazing to see the progression of acceptance to a point where currently, for the most part, people living with disability are now engaged in the community in positive and meaningful ways.

In our diagnosis journey, we went through many phases - a grieving phase, an "asking questions" phase, a " applying everything you learnt" and a "hoping for a miracle" phase. These phases were not experienced uniformly, instead, we weaved our way through the stages, returning to some on the way. This wasn't a quick process, it was a journey of roughly 15 years before some sort of peace and acceptance was affirmed within us, and our family. A large portion of our grieving process which came in waves over our journey was mourning the loss of what we thought our children's future would be and what our ideal family life would have been. Coming to the end of our long and continuing journey we have reached a point of acceptance. Seeing the beauty of what we have, accepting, and acknowledging each child's unique abilities and most importantly their valuable role within our family unit. While it was difficult to navigate the extensive process of grieving – without it – we would not have reached the stage of acceptance where we stand today.

Parent's Concerns Q & A

How will they learn?

Will other children accept them?

Will they have any friends?

How do we protect them & keep them safe?

How do we help them develop?

How can we both work?

How do we afford medications, treatments and therapy?

Are there other concerns that you think parents would have?

2 STAGES OF DIAGNOSIS

Diagnosis and the Stages of Grief:

The stages of grief are commonly observed in families following receiving a diagnosis for their child. A valuable resource for educators is an article produced by Parent Companion Organisation, on Understanding the Stages of Grief. (Understanding the Stages of Grief, n.d). For further and more in depth understanding and knowledge surrounding the psychological impacts of receiving a diagnosis a recommended reading is the article "The Impact of Childhood Disability: The Parent's Struggle" (Moses, 2004). Dr Ken Moses has conducted extensive research in the psychology field, specifically surrounding parent's experience with receiving and processing a diagnosis.

It is important to remember that the stages of grief are not linear, and parents may experience these emotions in a different order than the documented sequence, or they may return to stages.

Individuals may return to stages with the occurrence of each developmental milestone or a significant life event. This can trigger feelings of grief, depression, or denial. These feelings will at times arrive with the occurrence of what would generally be perceived as life events or milestones. Parents will reflect on the opportunities and experiences, they had imagined their child engaging in. Over time, these feelings and expectations diminish. They move through the stages of grief, into some level of acceptance, when these thoughts become framed more positively.

Parents even in their state of acceptance may reflect and engage in conversations about "I wonder if they would have played cricket?" or "Where would they be working?". These thoughts in the acceptance stage are more imaginative rather than focusing on what has been lost.

A summary of these stages adjusted to the experience of parents of a child living with a disability is provided in the graphic on this page.

In the initial years after my children's diagnosis, as an early childhood teacher, I thought that if I could read more books to them, do more craft activities, or sand play I could support their development. I had to realise that these activities are essential for children to engage in and aid in supporting sensory regulation they were not the quick or miraculous fix I was seeking. I had to come to terms with the fact that doing these activities could improve my sons' skills but not cure their disability.

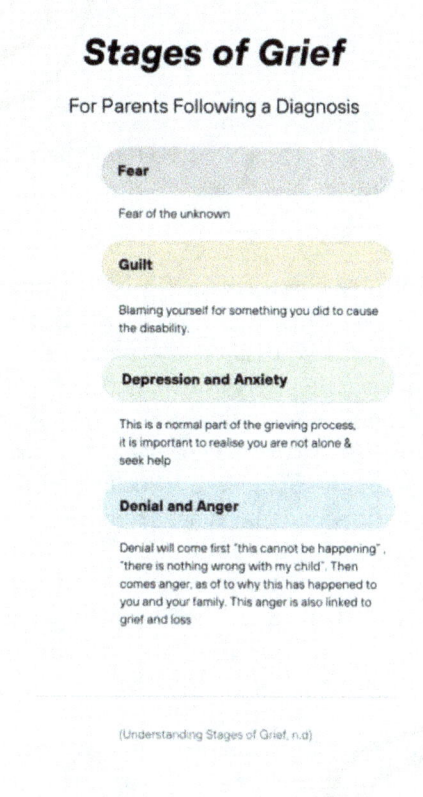

It is important to realise, despite wanting to do everything you read in an article or that a friend told you. The activities you may try are not the magic cure for your child's disability. However, rather than focusing on providing the magic cure, look at your everyday routine as a valuable tool in providing them opportunities to learn new skills.

Play is vital for children living with and without a disability. Play will still support learning, emotional and sensory regulation, whilst allowing children living with a disability to engage in learning experiences. As an educator, providing these experiences not only supports the child's development but also supports families indirectly, by providing their child with an inclusive, enjoyable environment and supporting them to develop new skills.

Whilst working with children living with a disability, one of the best things you can do is put yourself in the family's shoes. This allows you to think about how they feel and what they deal with day to day. This helps you to best support them throughout their child's time at your service.

How families move through the stages of diagnosis:

After receiving a diagnosis there are numerous stages that a family moves through. This can also include extended family as they too navigate the reality of the diagnosis and need to deal with the repercussions of the diagnosis.

As an educator, the most valuable action in your role is to support the families as they move through the stages of receiving and accepting a diagnosis. The best way you can support them is by simply having awareness about what they may be experiencing. This can be grief, frustration, and denial. Your ability as an educator to recognise the stages a parent or family may be going through, and the associated thoughts and feelings will aid you in delivering the support they need. The support provided may range from lending a listening ear or providing resources and information. The Early Years Learning Framework outlines that "children thrive when they, their families and their educators work in partnership to support their learning, development and wellbeing." (Australian Government Department of Education, 2022)

By providing a listening ear at pick up or drop off time or during any meetings that you have with the family, you can support them through the stage of grief they are currently experiencing. Allowing the family time to process their grief without too many questions or pressures about how therapy is going or how they are feeling is vital.

My Experience of the Stages of Diagnosis

These stages are in no way scientific; however, these are the stages that I as an individual, my immediate and extended family all went through following the diagnosis. I believe many other families, including those accessing your service, would experience very similar stages.

1. Why their child?
2. Wanting to resolve or fix it.
3. Acceptance
4. Seeing a future
5. Living their life

Stage 1. Why Their Child?

The first stage is a question of why - why their child, why their family, why is this so hard? These are questions that are not easily answered or that often have no answer at all. A time frame for this stage is difficult to predict. You may also find it difficult to support families in this stage, as you as an educator can also not provide them with an answer to their questions and confusion. During this stage as educators, it is best to listen and empathise.

Stage 2. They can fix it.

Parents will want to solve it. They become a 'super parent' trying to find a solution to make it better for their child and their family. They can become lost in the overwhelming number of options, suggestions, and opportunities provided to them as they try to find a solution.

Sometimes finding the solution becomes the focus of their life. This can be an isolating experience for them, taking up a lot of time, energy, and emotion. Families will often put a lot of time and effort into finding a solution for a disability, as there is so much information about how to support and manage those living with a disability. Many families will want to try anything that they can to 'fix' it. Finding the 'fix' can very quickly become the focus of the parent's or family's life. Copious research is involved in finding the 'fix', with families reading into this information, believing they have found the cure to the diagnoses. At times they can become so involved in this process and the offered solutions, that they lose track of other things occurring in the world around them, further isolating them. This focus becomes their life, placing large amounts of effort into researching and applying their latest knowledge. As a result, the 'fix it' stage can be very isolating, time-consuming, and emotionally exhausting.

However, over time, families will come to realise that there isn't always a cure or a quick fix. Management of disabilities can range from medical intervention, and medications or attending regular therapy or intervention services such as speech or occupational therapy.

With a diagnosis, often comes the need to regularly attend a range of medical and therapy interventions. This can take a huge toll on families. To attend the required appointments, their whole weekly routine changes. They are now juggling more things than they have before whilst still working through the stages of grief associated with receiving the diagnosis. Despite the amazing benefits of therapies, for these to be effective families must be consistent in attending their sessions, in conjunction with applying what is learnt in the home environment. This can be monotonous and draining for families. Taking all their free time after work or sibling school commitments by attending or completing therapy tasks. The demands of therapy can also be frustrating when you are in the 'fix it' mindset, wanting to be able to do everything you can for your child, whilst juggling your other family responsibilities. This can feel like a never-ending battle for families, trying to 'fix it', hold the rest of the family together and grieve all at once.

As educators, you must provide support to families during this stage. The best support is reassurance; letting them know they are doing their best and it is ok to sometimes not do it all or to do it perfectly. There can be days when it is too overwhelming to go to therapy or the child has a bad session. Support during these times may be as simple as a reminder of what their child achieved last week. Or just a welcoming smile and an "it's ok" can be enough to give them the energy to keep going.

This can also be a challenging time for siblings and is something to consider if you have multiple children from a family attending your service. Just like parents, siblings have also had significant changes in their lives. Some may not be old enough to comprehend the extent of the diagnosis and the significance of what has happened; however, they will likely be aware of changes in the family dynamic. With the increased need to attend therapy sessions, time normally spent with the siblings or enjoying activities as a family unit may be reduced.

As an educator, these children in your service may also need additional support. They may need reassurance throughout the day. This may come in the form of listening, a cuddle or knowing when to give them space. Acknowledging and accepting their negative or positive emotions justifies how they are feeling. This shows the child that they are accepted and supported.

Stage 3: Acceptance

The acceptance of a diagnosis happens in the parents' own time. This may take weeks, months, or years. It is also important to note that both parents will not progress through this stage at the same time. During every individual's journey to acceptance, they will feel many different emotions and see their child's disability through many different lenses. Slowly they will begin to see the beauty of the diagnosis and the amazingness of their child. The positive aspects of the disability and feel pride in their child's achievements.

As an educator, you will also begin to develop a new view of the child. You will appreciate their strengths, needs and quirks. Simply what they bring individually to your service. Some children will have excellent shape recognition and matching skills, an eye for details and a love for putting things together. This is the child you ask to help when the puzzle shelf is a mess of incomplete puzzles that need to be put back together. Completing these puzzles easily and knowing they are contributing to the tidiness and wellbeing of the room gives the child a sense of achievement, responsibility, and pride.

Their peers see this child's strengths and they may ask this child for help when they are having trouble finishing a puzzle. What a boost to the child's self-esteem! To be asked for help from a peer when they may often be rejected by their peers for being different, or due to their challenging behaviour. A win-win situation. Look for these opportunities throughout the day to create a safe and inclusive environment for children with or without a disability.

A part of the family's acceptance of the disability will be the development of a new "normal" routine.

This will most likely differ significantly from their previous routine, and it can be a stressful change for parents and siblings. This new routine may not look like what a family routine usually looks like, however, it works for the family and ensures the family can survive and even thrive. Aspects of these routines may seem strange or insignificant to those outside the family, but they must be adhered to. These routines can be a matter of life and death for some disabilities or be the reason why a child can stay calm and regulated so they can participate in everyday life.

Understanding the importance and accommodating these routines is essential for educators. When the routines are followed, it makes life at home calmer and smoother. This helps the transition into therapy or an early childhood service. This will also make their day at the service a more positive and calm experience for them and allow them to thrive. If there is understanding and consistency in the implementation of routines across a child's day, week, month, and year, then everyday life becomes more manageable for families.

When their child's routine is met with acceptance and understanding, it lightens a significant load and stress off the family. It is much easier for families when the importance of routines and consistency is understood and implemented, rather than having to argue for routines to be put in place. With new routines, comes additional and unnecessary stress for the family when asking for additional support to be implemented for their child. When requests made to educators or support services are met with understanding and consideration, it dramatically lightens some of the load the family is carrying.

ROUTINES

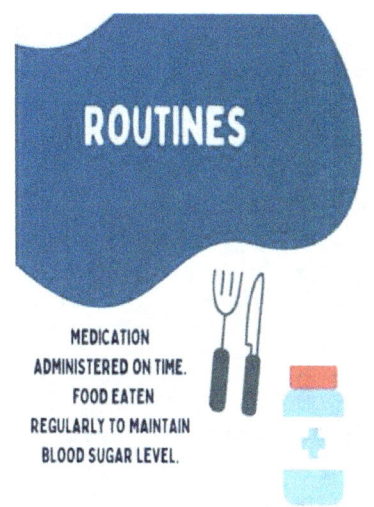

MEDICATION ADMINISTERED ON TIME. FOOD EATEN REGULARLY TO MAINTAIN BLOOD SUGAR LEVEL.

ALLOWING A CHILD TO USE THE SAME BLUE CUP EVERY DAY FOR THEIR JUICE MEANS THEY CAN COPE WITH THE DEMANDS OF THEIR DAILY ROUTINE.

LISTENING TO THEIR FAVOURITE MUSIC WHEN THEY ARE FEELING OVERWHELMED OR TIRED.

A TOY THAT IS SEEN AS A SECURITY OBJECT FOR THE CHILD IS ALLOWED TO BE ALWAYS WITH THEM.

Stage 4. Seeing a future

Parents will have a different vision of their child's future. This will constantly adjust as the child grows but there is a vision beyond the day-to-day. They will begin to see their child's strengths and appreciate the differences, opportunities, love and joy this child has brought into their life.

After moving through the acceptance stage, parents and family members move beyond the blur of receiving a diagnosis, learning about the diagnosis, and the exhaustion of medical and therapy appointments. They begin to look ahead to the future.

Stage 5. Living their life

The final stage is where we see families getting on with their lives, having adjusted to their new normal. Here they can value the experiences they have had and know their life is richer due to the experience of having had a child or children with a disability in their family. The routine that was once new and required conscious thinking to maintain, has now become a natural ebb and flow in their household and life. They have been provided with and implemented tools from therapists to support their child, themselves, and other family members.

They can now plan for a future that is theirs and adjust if they need to as complications arise. Parents and siblings of a child with a disability have a unique perspective on the world. One that you don't usually get to experience, taking the time to learn about this experience can benefit the way you teach and care for children.

Often families accessing an early childhood service are still in the beginning stages of seeking answers and solutions. If you have other families or educators who have been through diagnosis and have reached this stage of acceptance. Ask if they are willing to share their story, ideas experiences or advice, it is a perfect opportunity to support those parents who have recently received a disability diagnosis.

3 ACCESSING AN EARLY CHILDHOOD SERVICE

Early childhood services are just as valuable for those living with a disability, as those living without, supporting their development and school readiness. However, there are additional reasons that children living with a disability are encouraged to access a service:
- Advice from a therapist or medical staff
- The family will want their child to socialise and take part in a regular part of childhood.
- Financial reasons - both parents may need to work.

It is a stressful experience for most families when they choose to access an early childhood service. However, there are additional layers of stress when their child is living with a disability. There will be many concerns and fears. This is especially true for families who have not yet had a child attend an early childhood service. Engaging in these services can be an overwhelming experience. Parents must learn how another service or provider within the medical, disability or education space works. They also need to understand the expectations of the early childhood service.

Some of the concerns a parent may have.
- The educators don't know specific information about the disability.
- Educators don't have enough knowledge to understand and meet their child's needs.
- The correct procedure for administration of medication or feeding such as peg feeding.
- They don't know how their child will respond to a new routine or change.
- It is important to know that a change in routine can trigger changes in behaviour – often negatively.
- The child may have health issues. Does the positive impact

of socialising overcome the potential of being unwell or having medical complications?
- If the child is nonverbal and finds communication difficult it is even harder to let go. It is so frightening to think of their child being unable to communicate that they are hungry, thirsty, or tired or any other need they may have.
- An aspect of the disability is that the child may not tolerate anyone else caring for them.
- Challenging behaviours, due to the disability, may cause issues for the educators and other children at the service.

Completing all the paperwork that is required for enrolment is another huge job to complete. The number of forms, reports, and surveys you complete for your child is huge when your child has a disability. We had a filing cabinet drawer for each of our sons to keep their required paperwork. Compared to our daughter who had one small file that fitted in with the rest of ours. Paperwork overload is a real thing and as early childhood educators, it is something I am certain you can relate to!

Be patient with families completing this process and offer to take the time to assist them.

For families that have been through the diagnosis stages, the process of looking for and finding a service that can meet their child's needs can be confronting. Then the reality of sending their child to the service can be a stressful and fearful time. No one knows their child like they do. When there is an additional aspect of a disability, it makes it harder to trust that someone else can care for their child.

When a child is diagnosed while at the service you will have been involved in the diagnosis process. The educators may have been the people who encouraged the parents to seek a diagnosis. Later I discuss how to go about this process in a way that can best support both educators and parents. You will know the child quite well, but it is important to be aware that the child's behaviour can vary between the service and the family home. There is research on children holding it all in at the early childhood service or school and then letting it all out at home. The family is on the receiving end of negative behaviour at home, meaning the parent's and siblings' experience can vary greatly from what your experience is with the child. It is important to believe the parents and find ways to support them through the process, rather than adding judgement or belittling their experience.

With this new perspective of what parents are dealing with - and how they may be feeling - you can brainstorm some ideas with your colleagues to support the families

BRAINSTORM
HOW YOU CAN SUPPORT FAMILIES AT YOUR SERVICE

SOME SUGGESTIONS TO HELP YOU

TAKE SOME TIME TO STEP INTO THE PARENTS' SHOES

LEARN ABOUT THE DISABILITY

READ BOOKS WRITTEN BY PARENTS OF CHILDREN WITH A DISABILITY

THINK OF HOW DIFFICULT THIS STEP IS FOR THEM

IDENTIFY SMALL WAYS THAT YOU CAN HELP TO MAKE IT A LITTLE BIT EASIER

4 SUPPORTING CHILDREN IN YOUR SERVICE

Prior to starting at the service

You must meet with the family to explore their needs and expectations - and clarify your expectations.

Family Expectations

- Their child needs to attend to improve their social skills and develop friendships.
- Medication is given at regular times.
- A record of medication being given
- Routines need to be implemented and maintained.
- Daily communication with parents - and this can be more in depth than your usual end of the day conversation.
- Communication with therapists
- Incorporating therapy as part of the child's routine
- Assistance with self-help skills such as toileting.

Educator Expectations
- Parents provide a clear routine so they can meet the child's needs.
- All items e.g., dummy, snuggly, and medical equipment are provided.
- Instructions for use of medical equipment.
- Lessons on using the medical equipment.

To ensure the enrolment runs smoothly, it is important to recognise and validate the concerns that parents may have. During early conversations, it is important to understand where the family are at in their journey of receiving and living with a diagnosis. Listen to their story without judgement and ask questions. Build a broad picture of the family and why they want or need to enrol. Building this understanding will develop trust and rapport, allowing families to feel comfortable when enrolling their child at your service.

Being open and compassionate will be the basis for a strong working relationship with the family. A strong relationship between families and educators will help to deal with any issues when they arise and allow communication to flow freely when concerns or problems need to be discussed. When the family feels listened to, they will be happier, more open, and more likely to share information with you. They will feel comfortable to approach you with questions, concerns, or requests. This can assist their child to settle into, remain settled and engaged supporting their development and the wellbeing of all involved.

When both parties outline what they need or expect, educators can support the child and family in the way they need. The family will be aware of the educator's needs and expectations and what they can do within their role as an educator. This will build your knowledge and understanding, and help the family feel more comfortable about their child attending your service. Strong relationships and clear expectations of both parties ensure the best outcome for the child.

Collecting the correct information is crucial to:
1. Supporting the child's needs at the service
2. Supporting fellow educators
3. Supporting other children at your service
4. Supporting the family through adjustments and challenges

Remember, for parents, what may seem a small step or even an insignificant achievement for their child can be the result of many months of therapy and consistent hard work by their parents. Celebrate their child's achievements – big and small. Some examples to look for:
- Arriving happily at the service, smiling at others
- They put their hat on before going out to play without needing to be reminded or having a meltdown.
- They can help pack away resources.
- Can begin to feed themselves.

- Wash their hands independently.
- Interacts positively with another child.

Hearing these things can make all the hard work seem worthwhile and build the relationship between you and the family.

Recognising children's cues

It takes time to get to know a child's particular cues, even parents take time to recognise their children's cues. When they are sharing this very important information with you, ensure you take the time to listen.

Listening shows you respect the child and family and shows them you want to do your best to care for their child. It will also make your role as an educator easier when working with a child living with a disability. Until you know these cues it can be difficult to communicate with them and meet their needs. It may also be essential for the child's health as you may need to be able to notice the signs of ill health to prevent the child from becoming seriously unwell.

Two Perspectives – being a parent of children with a disability and an early childhood educator.

Juggling the parenting and professional aspects of being an early childhood teacher has been tricky.

My knowledge of disability has helped many families and educators, but it also raised my frustration when I could see educators still didn't understand where families were coming from. What the families needed to meet the needs of their child, hence the reason for this book.

I would get frustrated when families wouldn't respond to my own or my co-educator's suggestions regarding their child's development, however, I could always remember my reluctance to have a diagnosis for my children. This perspective allowed me to understand and empathise with families when other educators struggled.

My twin sons were 2 years and 3 months old at the time of diagnosis, I had returned to full-time work as a Director of an Early Childhood service so my husband, Tony could be a stay at home Dad to our boys and, our daughter before she started Kindergarten the following year.

Working at an early childhood service with a management committee consisting solely of parents was an advantage, as they were very understanding about my need to attend therapy appointments with our boys.

Each Monday during term time Tony, our son's and I attended the early intervention service playgroup. I also had the flexibility to attend other appointments as they arose. This roundabout of therapy or medical appointments is exhausting. At each appointment, you will have either therapy to do at home or decisions to make regarding medication, procedures or sometimes both.

Every family will experience something different.

Some families may only have one type of therapy to attend and implement while others may have therapy and medical issues. Some families may be juggling having three to four children attending different therapies or requiring medical intervention.

This roundabout of therapy sessions, appointments, decision making, and routines is exhausting and time consuming for parents and their families. The next time you approach one of your parents who has a child or children with a disability approach them with this perspective in mind. See if you can apply this new perspective to be more understanding, encouraging and supportive.

Therapy not only occurs during sessions but flows into home life. Parents will be asked by the therapist to complete activities and exercises sometimes with special equipment to support incorporation into their daily routines. When educators incorporate some of the therapy into the child's routine at the service this can lighten some of the load on overloaded families.

Educators can do this by incorporating therapy ideas into the child's daily routine at the centre. These may be simple things that you as an educator do every day but are so valuable in assisting families and children with therapy goals.

Doing speech therapy exercises during the day, these can be incorporated into play, routines or as part of group experience at the service.

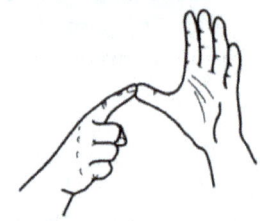

Sign language or Auslan can be taught to all children and educators.

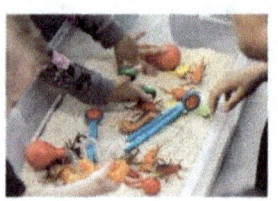

Providing therapy activities such as playdough to strengthen fine motor skills are part of the everyday at a service and children are doing their therapy without realising it, a win for everyone.

Role playing social interactions by educators during play is a valuable tool that all children can benefit from

When my children were diagnosed, my co-educators observed the impact of this life changing event firsthand. Their support and genuine concern and care for myself and my family were invaluable. My co-educators learnt from my personal experience. They saw the numerous appointments we attended and the decisions we made. This included lifestyle changes regarding medication, diet, and routine, and the way these affected our personal lives.

In the professional space, they observed the way I interacted with families dealing with diagnosis. To their credit and professional growth, they took the opportunity to learn from this and began to interact with families with a child living with a disability more positively.

They absorbed the information that I shared with them regarding the Autism Spectrum and the reality of receiving a diagnosis. This provided them with a different perspective that they otherwise would not have had, until another individual with personal experience, shared this with them. It comes back to walking in someone's footsteps until you have done it, and you can't understand it.

"You can't understand someone until you've walked a mile in their shoes."

Reflection Questions!

How would this make everyday life harder?
How would this affect parenting skills?
How would this affect relationships within the family?

I recently returned to this service to ask for input regarding this book. The openness and willingness to increase their knowledge and identify what they needed to learn helped to guide the content of this book. Their genuine desire to help children and families, made me feel reassured that the children and families would feel supported at this service. A positive aspect of having children who live with a disability, it gives you a different perspective that you can share with others and allow them to improve their teaching practice.

As I moved to other services the educators would always ask questions about my children, which was beneficial to both parties. It supported their learning and helped me to come to terms with our diagnosis as I talked it through and explored some of my feelings about my children's disability. It can be daunting to approach this type of conversation. This can help to build educators' confidence in working with families whose child has a disability.

Educators will have different experiences of disability due to their, age, experience, and backgrounds.

It can be difficult to deal with these situations as a new educator straight out of university or TAFE. The support of experienced educators around new educators does help. It can be daunting to approach a parent or family about their child's disability. To prepare for this during a room or staff meeting you could discuss the following questions.

Discussion points
- Is it ok to ask parents about the disability?
- What questions should you ask?
- Can you ask practical questions?
- Do you have a good enough relationship with this parent to ask difficult questions?
- Do you use the term disability, special needs or additional needs?
- Will using a term such as disability instantly put barriers up between you and the parent?
- Which term are you comfortable using?

The opportunity to talk to families newly diagnosed was a part of my role that I loved. I was able to help them through the haze of diagnosis by listening and talking about my experience. I could give them information about services or other ideas that educators didn't have.

Personally, sharing with those families that already had a diagnosis helped me share a burden or have a laugh about our family life. Sharing information that helped them gave me a boost because I was supporting them with my knowledge and experience. There were also numerous ideas or information that I received to help my family or the families within the service. Keeping the lines of communication open is so valuable for all educators.

As the Director of a service, I was able to help other families with children with a disability to feel comfortable in enrolling their child into the service. They felt comfortable enrolling their child at the service as they knew I had lived experience and "I got it". I was able to help them connect with other disability services and provide practical ideas. Most importantly be a listening ear and someone who could understand their situation. For those parents, it was so important to feel that they were heard and the challenges they faced were acknowledged and validated.

Personally, and professionally, I found it hard knowing some families didn't have the skill to advocate for themselves or their children. They didn't know how to access services or access funding. This process has been made easier for families since the introduction of the National Disability Insurance Scheme (NDIS) in Australia as the funding application process before the NDIS was difficult. You had to know who to talk to, use their terminology and jump through numerous hoops to apply for the funding.

Put simply, families with low literacy and communication skills, low confidence, or the inability to go into the community due to the restrictions of the disability to meet with these organisations missed out. The National Disability Insurance Scheme (NDIS) funds people with a disability to access services and supports they require to develop their highest level of independence while engaging with services within their community. The NDIS provides so many opportunities for people with a disability, however, you still need the skills to advocate for the person who requires the funding or for yourself if you have a disability and are in the position to advocate for yourself. There is paperwork that needs to be completed by doctors and therapists to support the application to ensure you can be funded at the level you need. To apply for the NDIS, you can make a verbal application by phoning 1800 800 110 or completing an Access Request Form. For assistance, you can also contact your local area coordinator, early childhood partner or a local NDIA office.

Advocacy was a big part of our lives for our children as well as advocating for others. Early childhood educators are always advocating for children in their care. Implementing the suggestions in this book you can advocate for them to receive the best from their NDIS plan by understanding the purpose of the NDIS Early Childhood Early Intervention (ECEI) funding.

NDIS and Early Intervention

NDIS Early childhood intervention is all about giving children with developmental delay or disability, and their families, support to enable the child to have the best possible start in life.

Assisting families to understand how to use their child's funding to support school readiness is an important role that you can provide. I have developed a resource aimed at parents, titled Understanding Your Child's NDIS Plan. This resource is beneficial for educators to provide to families to aid them in understanding their NDIS plan and how to best utilise funding to support school readiness. Please find the link to this resource at the bottom of the page.

https://www.carersaustralia.com.au/information-for-carers/early-childhood-intervention/

What is the reality of being the parent of young children with a disability and working in an early childhood service?

One difficult aspect of working within an early childhood service when my children were first diagnosed was seeing the children at the service meet the developmental milestones that my children weren't meeting. I remember an educator rushing into the office to tell me "Will did a wee on the toilet". He was younger than my children at the time and they should have met this milestone 12 months before this child but hadn't. While I was excited and happy for the child who had met his milestone on time (or even earlier) – I will admit my heart sank and I thought why can't my children do that?

As time goes by you accept the reality of this and adapt to recognising the tiny milestones. So, remember not to overlook them, for any child learning to feed themselves can be an achievement. For a child with a disability picking up the spoon can be as big an achievement as a child without a disability putting that spoon into their mouth.

Celebrate the tiny achievements. Parents want to hear their children being celebrated. It is hard to see and hear what all the other children are achieving when your child is working so hard to meet their milestones.

For parents and families of a child living with a disability, advocating and advocacy are constant. As the child grows, every stage of development requires new supports and ideas to be implemented. There are so many different areas to advocate in - medical, social engagement, inclusion and equipment needs. This results in developing new skills and to think outside the box. For me, this also flowed into my work as an early childhood teacher. I sourced some excellent resources and opportunities for the service through my disability advocacy skills. There have been many positives from my son's diagnosis that have supported my role as Director or Teacher at an Early Childhood Centre and Head of Department at TAFE.

5 HARD CONVERSATIONS, STRATEGIES, AND TECHNIQUES TO SUPPORT FAMILIES.

As an educator how do you have those hard conversations with parents and families? The conversations where you raise your concerns about their child's development or behaviour. No one ever wants to hear their child is not developing as they expected and hoped they would. As the educator who needs to initiate this conversation, it is not an easy conversation to have and not one that you look forward to.

Unfortunately, there is no bulletproof answer.

Successfully holding this type of conversation is a skill I have developed over my 30 years of working in the early childhood sector. Not all these conversations have ended with the outcome I wanted as parents aren't always willing to listen. However, I could walk away from the conversation knowing I had done my best for the child concerned and met all my professional responsibilities. I will share my tips, ideas, and suggestions with you to help you through these tricky conversations. I acknowledge how frustrating it can be when parents don't or won't listen.

The Type of Conversation:

It is important to first consider the context and purpose of the conversation. Consider:
- Is the conversation with the family of a child who doesn't yet have a diagnosis?
- Do you want to have this conversation because you have concerns about their developmental delays and want to bring these to the family's attention? Or
- Is it a family who already has a diagnosis and you need to talk to them about an issue that has arisen?

There are some points to consider before you have any conversation.
- The relationship you have with the family. Are they a family that is new to the service? Or is it a family that has other children attending the service and you already have a good rapport with them?
- Are they a parent that easily accepts feedback about their child or children?
- Are they a parent that is easy to approach when you have issues to raise with them? Have you had to raise issues with them before?
- Is it a new family and you haven't had time to build a rapport with them or know how they will respond to this type of conversation?
- Is one parent in the family easier to talk to than the other?
- If the parent is a sole parent is there a support person for them, who may help during the meeting? Or who may be more open to the conversation?
- Is there an educator at the service that the parent/s have a good relationship with and this educator may be the best person to begin this conversation?

How Do You Prepare for This Initial Conversation:

- Prepare notes or a mental checklist about what you want to say,
- Make sure you have your documentation ready (more on this later)
- Have you talked about your concerns with another educator, room leader or director of the service?
- How do you start the initial conversation about your concerns? – see examples below
- Where will you have the meeting?
- Does it need to be formal and held in a meeting room? Or is a more informal conversation in a setting such as the playground a more appropriate place for this conversation?

Content of a Casual Initial Conversation:

You can start the conversation by saying,
"Hi, I noticed Joey has been covering his ears a lot during the day to block out noise."

"Hi, I noticed Lucy was absorbed in her play today and lining up the cars in a row, does she do this a lot at home?

"Hi, I noticed James didn't respond when I was talking to him today and he didn't respond to the other educators either, has he done the same thing at home?"

"Hi when Emily was trying to climb the climbing frame, I noticed she had trouble coordinating her arms and legs. Does she do much climbing when you go to the park?"

The response from the parent will let you know if they are receptive to your concerns.

A responsive parent may agree with you and say, "Yes, I have noticed that lately, he has been covering his ears a lot/not responding when we speak to him. I will make a doctor's appointment to see if he has an ear infection." It is important to acknowledge their willingness to attend to this matter, ask them to keep you updated and let them know you will keep an eye on this at the centre too.

Following these guidelines can assist you in having a positive initial conversation that will help both the educator and parents explore the possibility of a child receiving a diagnosis.

A non-responsive parent may respond by saying "Joey is fine. His cousin does that too, he always has his hands over his ears, and he is perfectly fine".

If this is the response you receive, you should simply acknowledge what they have said. You could respond by saying "That's ok, I just wanted to let you know", then bring up something positive about his day to end the conversation. This way you have opened the door to communication and shown you won't barge through if they are not willing or ready to hear. Next time, they may be prepared to listen when you raise your concerns but for now, you have shown you care for their child and that you respect them.

Other responses could be:

"I was concerned he may have sore ears or maybe an ear infection I can keep an eye on it for you if you like?'

"Does his cousin not like loud noises?" or "How old is his cousin"? or "Is that the cousin that came with you to pick Joey up last week?"

Responding in this manner can help you build some rapport, using this as a basis when you do have hard conversations. These are techniques you may already implement. It can be hard to remember them when you have reached the stage of feeling frustrated that parents are not listening to you. It can be hard to remember the obvious when you are frustrated and instead focus on the fact that they are not listening to you.

These conversations can also make you feel nervous especially if it is the first time you have had this type of conversation with a parent. I have never found these conversations easy and would always be nervous beforehand.

Acknowledging that these hard conversations are difficult for both educators and families is important. Remember, you are both trying to do what is best for the child. At all times what is best for the child is the core of any interactions or conversation. If there is no recognition or acceptance of your concerns, then you will need to brainstorm some ideas of how you can move forward to best support the child.

How Do You Plan to Move Forward:

- Document your observations of the child's behaviour and development.
- Document further interactions with the parent if relevant.
- Talk to other educators who may have ideas or have been through a similar situation.
- Contact organisations such as KU Inclusion to ask for their support or ideas.
- Source support services – local early intervention services.
- Research the concerns that you have
- Talk with educators in the room and together put some strategies in place. Let all educators know what has been put in place – and support the implementation of these strategies when they engage with this child.
- Record what is happening so this can be evidence for a formal meeting or for any professionals who may later work with the child.

How Can You Help the Child in the Meantime:

- Implement the strategies you have developed consistently.
- Focus on the child's strengths and interests then use these to engage with the child.
- Remember that behaviour is not personal it is a form of communication. Don't take the child's behaviour personally.
- Implement routines and communication strategies to support the child, other children, and educators in the room.

Informal Conversation – progressing from the initial casual conversation:

You may start this conversation with parents by saying you have some concerns; do you have time to talk, or can we organise a time to talk?

Simply outline your concern and give an example if you have a long list just touch on one or two. You will know the parent so choose what you think they will respond to.

Example 1

"Sally is finding it hard to engage in play with her peers, she doesn't read their cues and finds it hard to share the equipment, in the home corner. She always wants to have all the cups and saucers so the other children can't play. When they ask for a turn, she shakes her head and gathers them all to herself. The children have stopped trying to play with her, so she is playing on her own".

Example 2

An 11-month-old baby is not yet crawling, and they aren't showing any interest or ability to raise themselves onto their knees to begin the crawling movement. They use a rolling motion to move around the room. Asking how the child moves around at home would start the conversation by raising your concerns about the delay in beginning to crawl.

If the parent is responsive to this conversation, you can ask further questions to gain a better understanding of the child in their home or social environments. This may also trigger some questions from the parents.

Sometimes we see the things our children do as normal, especially if this is their first child. Your questions could support and encourage the parents to look further into this or be a relief as they or a family member may have had concerns. If the parents have been in a stage of denial regarding their child's development or behaviour, this conversation can be the key to "giving" them permission to consider their child's development.

- What is their behaviour like with siblings or friends?
- Do they take turns at home?
- Do they rely on being picked up and carried at home?

If there is acceptance of your comments you could talk about

- Steps to move forward.
- Who to contact?
- Record any issues you see.
- Ask for ongoing feedback from home.

Suggest something that may help i.e., playing balancing games, ball throwing when they go to the park, services that may be able to help if that's appropriate. You can suggest ideas about organisations they could contact and where to find info websites some general and some specific i.e. Autism, ADHD, Downs Syndrome, Cerebral Palsy

How Do You Prepare for the Initial Meeting or Formal Conversation:

Have your documentation ready:

- Observations
- Summative assessments
- Checklists. I know they are frowned upon, however sometimes once a parent sees where their child is and where they should be this can be an incentive to act. All positive areas would be highlighted in this conversation, and you would start with the positives and use stories about the child as examples of what they are achieving then move into where you have concerns.
- Consider where you will have the meeting, you both need to be comfortable and have no interruptions.
- Space is always an issue in early childhood services but recently services have been designed with a meeting space in mind for this type of conversation. Those that haven't been designed that way are adaptable and can find a space to have this conversation.
- Time of day for conversation. Some things to consider here are parent work hours, the availability of the educators who need to be involved, the routine of service at this time and the availability of space.
- Who will be at the meeting? This a decision for each family, educator, and service, below are some things to consider before the meeting:
- Are two educators too confronting, is it better to have just one educator the parent is familiar with or are two people, ok?
- Does the educator having the conversation feel they need another educator there for support?
- Will the parents listen better if there are two educators?

Waiting for a Diagnosis:

In the meantime, while you are waiting for a child to receive a diagnosis. There are a range of things you can do:

- Continue to keep the communication lines open with the family.
- Research how you can support the behaviours that the child has and implement the strategies.
- Reflect on your teaching strategies and pedagogy – this is discussed in further detail in Chapter 8.
- Research services available to support parents, an example is Carers Gateway or access early intervention funding for the service to to employ an additional educator.

Often a disability that will be diagnosed when children are attending an early childhood service will be Autism, ADHD, speech delays or an intellectual delay. Other disabilities will sometimes be diagnosed earlier either before or after birth. Increasing your knowledge about these disabilities and services available and how to support children with these disabilities allows you to support the child and family while waiting for an official diagnosis.

Some points to remember:

- Parents will always want their child to be seen for who they are.
- Parents want to feel that they are heard and that their point of view is considered. Their circumstances, feelings and ideas must be taken into consideration.

Early Intervention

When it is recognised that a child may have a delay in their development health professionals or early childhood educators may suggest the child access an early intervention program. An early intervention program provides specialised support and services for children aged 0-7 who display signs of or have been diagnosed with developmental delay or disability. Accessing this service and the therapeutic interventions provided can have a positive impact on the child's development and the family.

Engaging in early childhood intervention services allows the child the opportunity to practice the skills they need to strengthen. It allows parents to learn how they can support their child to practice these skills in the home environment.

Parents must understand the importance of early intervention. You can and should play a large part in this by regularly engaging parents in conversations about their child's development.

Each state in Australia and each country has different early childhood intervention services. The way they are set up and run will vary greatly. To lessen confusion, seek advice and information from organisations such as Carers Australia. Carers Australia is an organisation that provides information to parents, family members, carers, and educators to help promote the development of each child, supporting them to reach their full potential. They can also assist in sourcing services in your local area, please find the link at the bottom of this page for access to this service.

Discussion Points

- Is it ok to ask parents about the disability?
- What questions do you ask?
- Can you ask practical questions?
- Do you have a good enough relationship with this parent to ask difficult questions?
- Do you use the term disability, additional needs, or special needs?
- Will using a term such as disability instantly put barriers up between you and the parent?
- Which term are you comfortable using?

6 SUPPORTING YOURSELF AND YOUR TEAM

I understand the frustration that comes when you raise your concerns with parents, and they just brush them off or respond negatively. I can recall having a family that did this. The ECT and I met with the parents and outlined our concerns.

The developmental delay wasn't significant but early intervention would have been a positive step for this child. The parents said, "She's a bit different" "It's just her" The mother said, "My mum said I was like that, and I turned out fine". The family decided not to access early intervention services although this was strongly advised by myself and the early childhood teacher.

Several years later, when the child was in third grade, I the saw mother and we had a chat about her child. The mother mentioned her daughter was really struggling and still had ongoing reading recovery support. This is an example of a situation where intervention and support would have made a significant positive difference to this child's development.

How do you Prevent Yourself from Getting Frustrated?

- Step into the parents' shoes, and recall the information provided in the first few chapters. The fear of receiving a diagnosis or the impact that the diagnosis can have.
- Take this understanding of how parents may be feeling into the conversations and meetings you have with families.
- Talk with your colleagues and express your frustration, feelings, and concerns about the situation.
- Try different tactics, information can be provided in different ways. Everyone learns or absorbs information differently so maybe a newsletter or video may help parents accept the information rather than a conversation.
- Self-reflection. Ask yourself, why is this an issue for you? Why are you frustrated? What can you do to relieve that frustration? Also, remember your self-care.
- Self-care can be exercise, a chat with a friend or a family member, socialising with family or friends, meditation, or exercise. Whatever makes you feel good will help you deal with this frustration and support your work overall.
- Communication skills – do you need to improve your communication skills so that you are expressing your concerns clearly? Ensuring the families understand what you are telling them.
- Reflect on what you have done to support the child and know that you have done your best to support the child.
- Focus on supporting the child. This is an area where you can have a positive impact and know that each day you have worked to your highest level to help them achieve and develop.
- Find information that may help you support the family and allow them to be open to what you are sharing with them.
- Establish a communication system with the family.
- Understand that by taking the leap and starting the conversation, a seed has been planted and you have taken the first step in seeking support for the child.

How do Leaders Prevent Frustration in their Team?

- Make sure the educator is prepared for the meeting and offer support by checking in, so they feel confident and that someone recognises the work they are doing to support the child and family.
- Ensure the educators speaking to parents feel supported after the conversation or meeting with a family. Check in with them so they can debrief, allowing them to share their success or their frustration.
- Remember to touch base on those difficult days when things have not run smoothly in the room for whatever reason. They may just need someone to talk to and express their concerns and frustration – I always found chocolate works wonders as well!
- Access information for them that will help them during the conversation with families or simply when working with the child.
- Source services that can provide ideas and support whether these are online or locally based.
- Encourage them to continue the conversation with the family and offer support for future conversations. It may be effective if the Director and the educator have the next meeting with the family.
- Be prepared to step in if you need to.

Team Collaboration

To ensure a room runs smoothly your educators must communicate with each other when they are discussing concerns regarding a child. Communication must always be clear and respectful. They need to keep each other updated on
- Concerns
- Incidents
- Conversations with parents
- Questions from parents
- Questions or concerns from other children's parents
- Effective communication methods

Inform other educators throughout the centre what you are implementing for this child. It is also important to make sure any casual staff are aware, so they implement the identified practices into place.

Routine is super important for the children and the educators. When the educators know what to expect from one another and implement the routine, the children also know what to expect. All children need consistency and routine in their lives. For children on the Autism Spectrum, this is even more essential. Educators need to work together to ensure the routine is consistent and also discuss what will happen if there is a change in routine. They need to have some strategies to cope with these times when the routine needs to be changed to support those children that don't cope (sometimes there are even educators who struggle with change in routine so also consider their needs)

Show appreciation – so many small ways you can do this – examples that have worked.
- A note of appreciation
- Positive feedback
- Recognition of their work during a staff meeting or to management

Most importantly remember to laugh, humour makes everything seem bearable. It will create a nicer environment for staff and children and ensure you have some fun moments during your day.

7 PARENT REACTION AND PARENT STORIES

Every parent will react differently.

Some want it straight and are open to what you tell them, others don't want to hear what you have to say. You have the skills to implement numerous teaching strategies for the personalities that you have in your room so remember to employ these when speaking with parents.

Remember at the core it is the child that is most important so put aside your beliefs of how the parents should react and focus on the best outcome for the child.

The experience of diagnosis and raising a child living with a disability can place a lot of pressure on you as an individual, your relationships, and the family dynamic. Raising a child living with a disability comes with a range of additional demands to meet their support needs. This may include attending therapy appointments, managing behaviours of concern, facilitating their integration into the community, and managing dietary requirements, just to name a few. Due to these demands and considerations, parents and their relationship are placed under significant pressure. Sadly, the build-up and ongoing nature of this pressure commonly leads to separation or divorce. It has been documented in both research studies and surveys, that the rate of divorce is significantly higher among parents who have a child living with a disability. A study conducted by Leimbach (2006) highlighted that the rate of divorces is 4 out of 5 among families with a child living with Autism.

A research study has examined the variance in divorce rates among the general population and those raising children living with disabilities. The below graph captures the findings of this study, as you can see divorce rates are significantly higher, with the average rate of divorce among the population sitting at 50%, increasing up to 80% for families raising a child living with a disability (Downing, 2006).

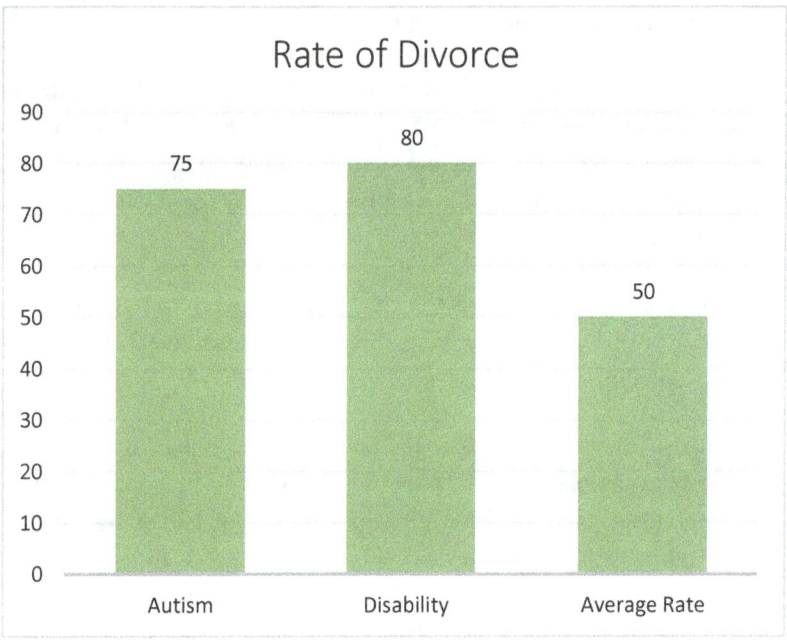

Parent Diagnosis Stories:

At around 18 months of age, we began to see changes in the Dalton we knew and loved. Dalton began to show repetitive behaviours; tapping his fingers on his knees, spinning, and twirling with his head tilted to the side, an apparent loss of awareness of his surroundings and to our voices. Dalton ceased to say Dad anymore and began to be completely nonverbal. Dalton was diagnosed at 2 years 10 months 8 days of age with severe autism, level 3: requiring very substantial support for deficits in social communication and very substantial support for deficits in restricted, repetitive behaviours. I felt relief in finally having a diagnosis yet felt a deep sadness for what life will now hold for Dalton. The tears began to roll down my cheeks, I sobbed and cried my heart out, this was a different type of grief I wasn't prepared for.

- KD - Mother of Dalton 6 years

My daughter was 7 when she was diagnosed autistic. I went through the gamut of emotions when I first received the news. Shock, disbelief, grief, and relief. Relief was a big one! I had been struggling to understand her behaviour for years. Was it a developmental phase? Was she autistic? ADHD? ODD? Was it my parenting? That was probably what I lost the most sleep over, wondering what I could do differently. So, it was a relief to finally have an answer…. of sorts. It's been a steep learning curve for me. I wasn't very knowledgeable about autism and as we all know, every autistic kid is very different so there aren't any easy answers. I've found reading and listening to autistic voices invaluable. It allows me to get inside my daughter's head somewhat and allows me glimpses into her world while she is still developing the vocabulary to articulate her experience.

- LE - Mother of Maisy 10 years

Receiving Cody's diagnosis was a shock to us as nothing had been picked up in all previous scans. Cody was my third child and due to my middle child being of a large birth weight and Cody was measuring ahead of time, they sent me for a sizing scan at around 31 weeks. I knew something was wrong during this scan as the chatty ultrasound operator went quiet, we were told we had to go see the clinic at the hospital that afternoon.

My husband and I sat nervously waiting to be seen by the Doctor. During the appointment, there were phone calls made to Canberra Hospital for arrangements to be made for us to go see the Foetal Medicine Unit, all while we were told nothing other than there may be an issue with my baby. The wait for this appointment to come around was extremely stressful. During our appointment with the Professor in Canberra, I had another Ultrasound.

We were told that they were 99% sure our baby had Down syndrome, a heart condition, a bowel condition as well as many other concerns. I was to go home to be monitored and return to Canberra the following week for further testing. I had an amniocentesis and had to stay close to the hospital that night in case I went into labour. I returned to the hospital the next day to have the baby's heart monitored, it was here they decided to admit me into the hospital with a wait and see while monitoring.

My husband returned home to be with our other children but had not been home long when I was visited by a room full of Doctors'. I was informed that my baby's heart was failing and was told to make the decision of letting him go or undergo an emergency c-section at 33 weeks.

We needed to give him a chance.

I was all alone in surgery but surrounded by an amazing surgical team who made sure I was okay every step of the way.

Embracing Disability in Early Childhood

Cody was taken away very quickly after birth, and I was unable to see him until the next day.

We soon discovered how sick he was.

Cody's diagnosis was now confirmed. He was born with Down Syndrome but with major health complications including being born with Transient Leukemia and the previous bowel and heart conditions that were suspected the previous week. To us, Cody having Down Syndrome was not a huge deal, we just wanted him to overcome all his health issues. In the coming days, we met with lots of specialists, most were amazing, but we also had some negativity.

One in particular, made us question our decisions by telling us that most people would have made the choice to let him go because people who have Down syndrome have an awful life.

Well, he is now 18 and having an amazing life surrounded by people who adore him and we watch him take on life with such determination and strength.

Our life wouldn't be complete without him.

- CM – Mother of Cody 18 years

8 EARLY INTERVENTION, SUPPORTS AND PEDAGOGY

NDIS and Early Intervention

NDIS Early childhood intervention is all about giving children with developmental delay or disability, and their families, support to enable the child to have the best possible start in life.

The NDIS provides funding to young children through early childhood intervention. The funding provides opportunities for infants, young children, and their families. This funding allows for individuals and families to access specialised supports and services they otherwise would not always be able to access due to cost. These therapy services aim to promote the following:
- child's development
- family and child's wellbeing
- a child taking part in their community.

Sometimes families cannot see the connection between their NDIS funding and preparing for school. The therapies that a child access through their funding can all work on school readiness skills. The link to my resource Understanding Your Child's NDIS Plan is below, at the bottom of the page for your provision to families.

Referral Process:
Knowing who to refer to is difficult. Each state in Australia has a different system of early intervention. The support provided can change depending on whether it is an urban, rural or remote area. There will generally be an early childhood early intervention program in your state.

https://innovativedisabilitysolutions.squarespace.com/store/p/your-childs-ndis-plan

Allied Health Therapists:

This includes physiotherapists, occupational therapists, or speech therapists, , which can be accessed through community health services. Children can be referred by their early childhood service, a general practitioner, and their parents. This referral process can be difficult for families who have English as a second language, due to numerous forms needing to be completed. If you as an educator/service can complete this process for them, it can be a godsend to the family and ensure that children can access these services. Enabling equal access for all children and families to these services is vital to their wellbeing and ensures the appropriate therapies are accessed to support their development.

Increasing your knowledge of Disability

Language – what words do you use when talking about disability?

The words or terminology since my children were diagnosed have changed. Initially, it was special needs, then additional needs and now disability or a person living with a disability. As a parent, I prefer the term disability or living with a disability. I feel as though I am not hiding who my children are and that I am saying loud and proud they have a disability, they are different and unique, and I love them just as they are.

Neurodivergent is a term that is preferred by some people in the Autism and ADHD space. Neurodiversity refers to the diversity of human minds. It describes the range of differences in individual brain functioning and behaviour, regarded as part of the variance in human populations. (Australian Government Department of Education, 2022)

It is recommended to use first person language for example Zac is living with a disability, and a recommended resource has been developed by the Victorian State Government. Please see the link at the bottom of this page.

https://www.vic.gov.au/state-disability-plan/our-language/person-first-and-identity-first-language#

What words do you use when speaking to children about disability? Firstly, you need to feel comfortable with the words you are using otherwise your discomfort will show and the children subsequently will feel uncomfortable and wonder what there is to worry about. If you lack confidence in engaging in these conversations, you could talk to parents, colleagues or research terms that are used. You could look further into the child's diagnosis and aim to use terms used within that disability that are appropriate.

There are two references to children with a disability in the glossary of the Early Years Learning Framework (Australian Government Department of Education, 2022).

Additional needs: the term used for children who require or will benefit or be able to participate more fully from specific considerations, adaptations, or differentiation of any aspects of the curriculum, including resources and the environment.

Children living with a disability: disability is part of human diversity. Many kinds of disability can result from accidents, illness, or genetic disorders. Disability may affect mobility, ability to learn, ability to communicate, or ability to engage with others and with experiences. Some children may have more than one type of disability. A disability may be visible or hidden, may be permanent or temporary and may have minimal or substantial impact on a child's abilities.

Do either of these explanations resonate with you? Will you begin to incorporate the term "child or children living with a disability" into your conversations or when speaking with parents? Does this feel too confronting for you? How will this link to your teaching pedagogy?

There will be a time when you must discuss disability with children, generally regarding a child who is living with a disability. If at the time this child is sitting in front of you and relying on you to accept them for who they are, you need to be able to explain how to interact with them and you need to do this confidently.

When my daughter's friends were younger or other children asked questions about my son's disability, we would say "Their brain works differently from yours". With the easy acceptance of children, the majority accepted this, but others would ask deeper questions which would make me stop and think! But this was the easiest and simplest way to answer their questions at the time and felt a comfortable way of explaining our experience. Below, you will find some useful links to articles to assist you in researching how to approach and negotiate these conversations when talking to children about disability.

https://www.firstfiveyears.org.au/child-development/how-to-talk-to-children-about-disability

https://www.abc.net.au/everyday/helping-your-kids-to-not-be-awkward-around-disability/11739256

Pedagogy

There are many explanations of pedagogy in early childhood education, a simple definition is pedagogy is the "how" of teaching, therefore you need to explore how you support, engage, and teach children with a disability as part of your teaching practice.

The Early Years Learning Framework defines pedagogy as
"the art, craft, and science of educating. Pedagogy is the foundation for educators' professional practice, especially those aspects that involve building and nurturing relationships, curriculum decision-making, teaching, and learning." (Australian Government Department of Education, 2022)

To implement this definition of pedagogy about children with a disability, how do you build relationships with them?
- Do you find this easy or difficult?
- If it is difficult, why is it difficult?

If you do find it difficult
- What can you change in your teaching approach to children with a disability to improve your interactions?
- How does this affect your current approach to pedagogy?
- Do you need to change your or the service's pedagogy?

Further questions to reflect on
- Do you approach curriculum decision-making differently for a child with a disability? Should you approach it differently?
- How do you implement behaviour strategies positively within the curriculum?
- Do you implement appropriate teaching strategies to support children with a disability?

Teaching Strategies
When teaching, interacting, and engaging with a child living with a disability do you believe you need to change your teaching strategies? Some teaching strategies that you may implement daily are.

- Asking questions
- Explaining
- Scaffolding
- Speculating
- Inquiry
- Demonstrating

If you change your teaching strategies, how can you do this in a way that reflects equality and respect for them as a person?

A child may require more hand over hand support, or an experience needs to be modified. This increases the emphasis on you as an educator developing the skill of providing support without completing the learning experience or task for them. Does this sit comfortably with you?

Your pedagogy may contain the belief that children need to explore to learn, if a child living with a disability doesn't have the same capacity or interest in exploring how does this affect the way you set up learning experiences or how you engage with this child? Reflecting on your teaching strategies can build a robust pedagogy or change how you and your service engage with a child living with a disability.

The Australian government has reviewed the *Disability Standards for Education 2005*. Following this, they have produced, a standard for disability education, referred to as the Final Report of the 2020 Review of the Disability Standards of Education 2005.

The review discusses aligning educators in early childhood services with school standards.
- Are you aware of this review?
- Do you know what these standards are?
- Would this affect how you work with families, children, and colleagues if you had this information?

Australian Government Department of Education, Skills and Employment (2020).

Pedagogy and the "Hows" of Teaching - Reflection Exercise:

How do you individualise teaching pedagogies and strategies to ensure your service is inclusive?

How do you engage children with a disability in all learning experiences and routines? The Early Years Learning Framework poses the view of "Consider who is included and who is silenced by ways of working" (Australian Government Department of Education, 2022).

Are there aspects of your teaching that are silencing children with a disability throughout the day? Is this shown through your words, interactions or the learning experiences that are provided?

How do your interactions with a child living with a disability show other children how to interact appropriately and empathetically with that child?

How are your relationships with the parents of children with a disability?

How do you think children with a disability enhance your program or make your day more difficult?

How do you work as a team?

How do you implement strategies to support a child with a disability?

Some practices are recommended for children with a disability, one of these is reasonable adjustment. Within your daily practice do you implement reasonable adjustment?

How do you support access to learning experiences? How is this reflected in your pedagogy and everyday practice?

Do the daily actions and strategies that you implement show that you see children living with a disability as competent learners who are valued within the service?

Documentation needs to reflect that the needs of a child with a disability are met, are there ways that you show this in your documentation?

Some examples:
- Using sign language throughout the day and recording the child's engagement and response to this. Note areas where you need to learn more signs to support the child's interests, needs and routine.
- Teaching sign language to all children and how you have shared this with their families.
- Provide learning environments at a variety of heights for ease of access.
- Setting up a sensory space and the children's response to this, what worked well, what didn't, and the children that responded positively to this space.
- To support a child who finds social engagement difficult. Provide a learning experience for two children so they interact with one child to build up their confidence and skills in social interactions.
- Experiment with playing different types of music during the day to see how children with sensory processing disorder respond and document the children's response, behaviour and engagement with the environment, peers, and educators.

- Engagement from children when movement breaks have been incorporated into the routine. Has this helped concentration?
- The positive result of keeping a sensory/comfort toy with them throughout the day. Did this help with sensory and emotional regulation?
- Change the lunchtime routine to support children with a disability that limits their mobility by placing the bowl for empty dishes on the table rather than children carrying dishes to the food trolley.

As part of your pedagogy can you reflect on how your daily interactions show that you respect and value every child? You may ask a colleague to observe your interactions and give you feedback on your interactions.

What happens after diagnosis?

Practical steps

When you have a clear understanding of the steps after diagnosis you can support families. They may need advice or reminders about what should happen next as they may be too overwhelmed to know what to do next. This is where going back to the stages of diagnosis can help you support them.

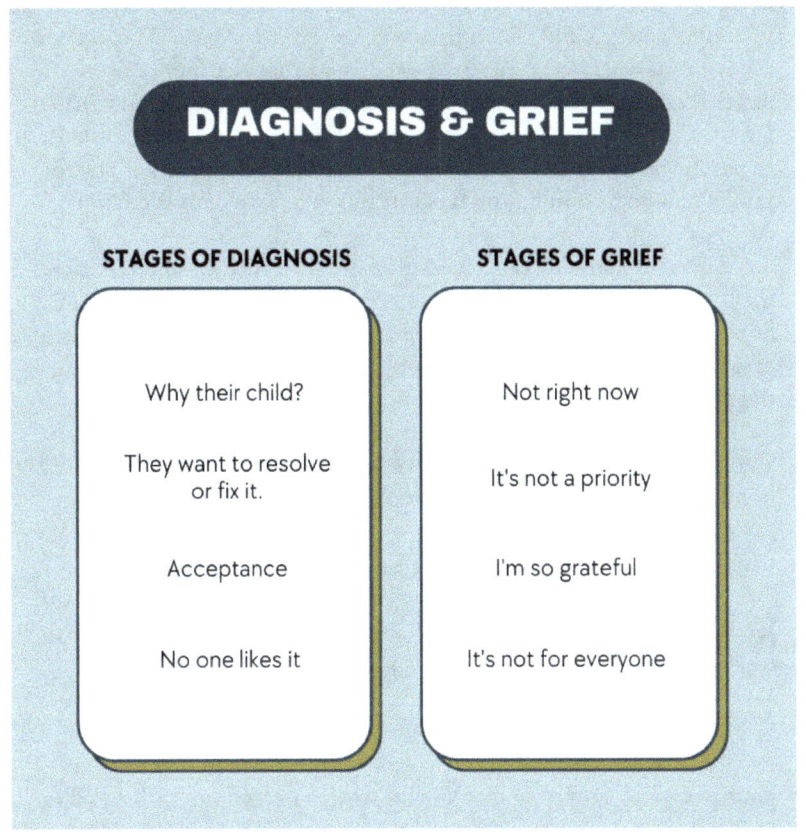

For children diagnosed with a developmental delay or a disability such as Autism, the immediate therapies will be speech and occupational therapy. Other diagnoses may require physiotherapy and other medical interventions. Quite commonly there are waitlists to access these therapies, especially in regional areas, meaning there are quite often delays in them starting these therapies. Waitlists are also common for accessing a pediatrician, a pediatrician is a doctor who specialises in children's health, in some cases, they can diagnose a disability or developmental delay. In some cases, families may wait anywhere from 18 months to 2 years to see a pediatrician.

While waiting to access therapies parents and families will be dealing with receiving a diagnosis and will want to do what they can to support their child. Then they will be told that there is a delay in accessing the service their child needs and that the family needs to make their everyday lives easier. This can be frustrating and make families feel angry. Any opportunities to link them to therapists or research what you can do to support them will be appreciated by the family and help to build the relationship you have with the family.

When the families can access therapists or medical intervention, they will be expected to fit these appointments into everyday life. Sessions can be weekly, fortnightly, or monthly and while this is a great practical step it does add an extra load onto already overwhelmed and busy families.

Families may have other children or both parents are working, be a sole parent family, or don't have family close by, whatever their unique situation is it is a difficult time.

This is a time of adjustment, and it can be overwhelming for families. This can be a reason why families may not respond to feedback that you are giving or may not want to be engaged in discussion about their child as it is just too overwhelming.

Step back and think about your approach to families currently, your pedagogy and how this links to your interactions with families and children.

How can you support the child's learning at this time?

Is it a time to be more hands on or hands off?

Do you need to learn new strategies to support the child's learning?

Therapy is a wonderful opportunity for children and their families, but it can also be very draining. Therapy isn't just an easy breezy session it is hard work for the child. They are completing tasks that they will find challenging to develop their skills.

To put it into perspective, think of that day when it is raining, you have your children with behaviour issues. A new child has their first day, and they are having difficulty settling in. An educator is away, and it is hard work to keep the room running smoothly – that's what therapy is like.

Children don't come out of a therapy session saying, 'Wow I feel fantastic!' They come out feeling tired, so educators and the family may see negative behaviour, tiredness, regression in development or a higher level of frustration in the child.

The child is giving 150% at each therapy session, the tasks they are given to do require so much concentration, and physical and mental effort that they can come away from a therapy session exhausted.

This can have ramifications on their behaviour which makes it difficult for families and the educators working with them. When a child returns from a therapy session, they may just need time to have some quiet space and readjust to being back in the busy environment of the early childhood service.

Attending therapy sessions gives more work to families:
- There are follow up activities or exercises to do at home.
- Decisions to make – for example which communication system to use, do they need to consider medication for their child, and what is causing sensory issues within the home? These can be some of the questions parents need to consider and there are many more.
- Purchases to make or finding ways to fund purchases.
- There can also be negative behaviours that come out of these sessions as children are working hard.

Overwhelming emotions:

In your role, you support children to deal with their emotions daily. Have a plan in place for this child when they re-enter the service after a therapy session. Will they need a cuddle and quiet time on your lap, a quiet space to gather themselves, time to run outside and work off the emotions of the session? Each child's needs will differ, so think of ways that can smooth their transition back into the routine.

The Educator's Role in Therapy

Early childhood educators can work with allied health therapists and professionals by implementing therapy in the service. The therapy tips shared with you may be a game to play that encourages language development or how to encourage a child to say a sound.

A communication book that therapists and family can write in allows information to be shared establishing a picture of what happens at the service, in therapy and at home. This supports all parties in developing routines and strategies to best support the child.

This is an opportunity to learn what the therapists are working towards and how they are doing it and it allows you to build your skills while supporting the child. A communication book builds the conversation and links between all the supports in the child's life. When you need documentation, a therapist will be more willing to provide it because you have made the effort to connect with them and acknowledge their role in the child's life.

9 SIBLINGS, THEIR ROLE, AND THE SUPPORT THEY NEED

The siblings of a child with a disability need to have their needs considered. In the busyness of therapy, medical appointments and a higher level of personal care that may need to be provided to a child or children with a disability, these siblings may have less of their parent's time and attention. The siblings in your care may need some time just to be themselves, to express themselves without thinking about disability or talking through what they are experiencing.

An effect of some disabilities is that the child with a disability has an interrupted sleep pattern, so other children in the family can be tired due to this. Understanding this and providing a quiet space can help to support the siblings. A space for the sibling to visit when they need a break or additional rest periods can work wonders to help support them as they adjust and cope.

The siblings within your care, need to be seen for themselves. At times for siblings, it can feel like their sibling's disability diagnosis is a cloud that follows them around. Children may want to express themselves, without this cloud and your service may be a safe space for them to do so.

It can be stressful, confusing, and overwhelming as the siblings adjust to new routines and changes to what was normal. They may want to talk through their experiences. The best thing you can do is to allow them to lead the conversation regarding these. Maintain a strong supportive relationship with them so they have someone there when they need them.

Older siblings, already known for being the third parent in most family dynamics, now have their parenting role amplified as they help with their sibling living with a disability and other children in the family unit. They will appreciate you acknowledging them for who they are as an individual. If they were attending your service before transitioning to school, they will appreciate that someone they are comfortable and familiar with understands their family dynamic and on drop offs and pick ups may appreciate a listening ear.

On a positive note, the siblings of a child with a disability adapt and become strong advocates for their disabled sibling/s. They will often find employment in the disability sector or study to move into one of the many therapy roles that people with a disability require. They are perfect in these roles as they have the lived experience these families and their children need. They are also some of the most caring, resilient, amazing human beings you will ever meet.

We worried our daughter was missing out on a normal childhood and tried to make up for it in lots of different ways. An educator needs to consider this, as sometimes this stress can be as much of a burden as the diagnosis. The need for strict routines for some disabilities also impacts negatively on siblings and creates difficulties for the adults in the family as well. We always found it hard to see our boys miss the milestones that our daughter had achieved. This can be something that affects the way parents accept information or feedback from you.

However, there have been so many positive outcomes for our daughter that we can say she is lucky to have siblings with a disability and we couldn't be prouder of the person she has become. The pride and passion demonstrated when she advocates for her brothers, and others within the disability community proves that lived experience is incredibly valuable. We can all take the opportunity to learn from this. It is difficult to meet the needs of a sibling who doesn't have a disability, and we constantly juggle our responsibilities in that area. When our daughter was in Year 12, I reduced my workload from full time to part time so I could spend some extra time with her before she left for university in another state. While at university she had her own business working as a support worker for NDIS participants. During this time, she received many positive comments from her clients. She is now a fully qualified exercise physiologist who is currently working with NDIS participants. We know we raised an amazing person, and we are very proud of her

RESOURCE LIST

Children's Books:

We Move Together by Kelly Fritsch

What Happened to You by James Catchpole & Karen George

Mama Zooms by Jane Cowen Fletcher

It was supposed to be Sunny by Samantha Cotterill

This Beach is Loud by Samantha Cotterill

Can Bears Ski? By Raymond Antrobus

I can talk like a River by Jordan Scott & Sydney Smith

Benji, the Bad Day or Me by Sally J Pla

Susan Laugh by Jeanne Willis

The Chalk Rainbow by Deborah Kelly & Gwyneth Jones

Just Because by Rebecca Elliot

My Brother is Very Special by Amy May

I See Things Differently – A First Look at Autism by Pat Thomas

My Brother Matthew by Mary Thompson

A Different Little Doggy by Heather Whittaker

All My Stripes by Shaina Rudolph

RESOURCE LIST

Websites for Further Information:

Autism Spectrum Australia
https://www.autismspectrum.org.au/

National Autistic Society
https://www.autism.org.uk/

Autism Speaks
https://www.autismspeaks.org/

Downs Syndrome Australia
https://www.downsyndrome.org.au/

Downs Syndrome Association
https://www.downs-syndrome.org.uk/

National Downs Syndrome Society
https://ndss.org/about

Cerebral Palsy Australia
http://cpaustralia.com.au/

Cerebral Palsy UK
http://www.cerebralpalsy.org.uk/

Cerebral Palsy Alliance Research Foundation
https://cparf.org

Epilepsy Action Australia
https://www.epilepsy.org.au/

Epilepsy Action
https://www.epilepsy.org.uk/

Epilepsy Foundation
https://www.epilepsy.com/

Diabetes Australia
https://www.diabetesaustralia.com.au/

Diabetes UK
https://www.diabetes.org.uk/

American Diabetes Association
https://diabetes.org/

PMFS Australia (Phelan-McDermid Syndrome)
https://pmsfaustralia.org.au/

PMFS UK (Phelan-McDermid Syndrome)
https://www.pmsf.org.uk/

Phelan-McDermid Syndrome
https://rarediseases.org/rare-diseases/phelan-mcdermid-syndrome/

Deafness
https://deafaustralia.org.au/

British Deaf Association
https://bda.org.uk/

National Association of the Deaf
https://www.nad.org/

Vision Australia
https://visionaustralia.org/

Royal national institute for Blind People
https://www.rnib.org.uk/

National Federation of the Blind
https://nfb.org/resources/blindness-statistics

National Organisation for Fetal Alcohol Spectrum Disorder
https://www.nofasd.org.au/

https://nationalfasd.org.uk/

Fragile X Association of Australia
https://www.fragilex.org.au/

Fragile X Society UK
https://www.fragilex.org.uk/

National Fragile X Foundation
https://fragilex.org/

Muscular Dystrophy Association
https://www.mda.org.au/

Muscular Dystrophy Association
https://www.mda.org/

References:

Australian Government Department of Education [AGDE] (2022). Belonging, Being and Becoming: The Early Years Learning Framework for Australia (V2.0). Australian Government Department of Education for the Ministerial Council.

Australian Government Department of Education, Skills, and Employment (2020). Final Report of the 2020 Review of the Disability Standards for Education 2005. Commonwealth of Australia.

Downing, R. (2006, March 2). Autistic in Tucson. Tucson Weekly, No page number.

Leimbach, M. (2006, March 5). Keeping it together: Parenting. The Sunday Times (UK), p.10.

Moses. K 2004, 'The Impact of Childhood Disability: The Parent's Struggle', PENT Forum, pp. 1-6, https://www.co.walworth.wi.us/DocumentCenter/View/3341/The-Impact-of-Childhood-Disability_The-Parents-Struggle

Understanding the Stages of Grief, n.d., Parent Companion Organisation, accessed 17 July 2023, https://www.parentcompanion.org/article/understanding-the-stages-of-grief

ABOUT THE AUTHOR

Jenny Nechvatal is an Early Childhood teacher with 30 years of experience in various roles within the early childhood sector in Australia. Jenny combines her knowledge of the early childhood sector and 21 years of lived experience parenting two children living with a disability. Teaching and Director roles within the sector involved working and supporting families who received a diagnosis of disability for their child either before starting at the service or while attending the service.

Using her personal experience, early childhood experience and leadership skills developed in various roles Jenny engaged with families to support them and provided a role model for educators to engage with and support parents as they trod the path of diagnosis and beyond.

Jenny has contributed a chapter to A Carers Journey, stories from the Heart, and writes a blog at Innovate Support Coordination and Innovative Disability Solutions. Jenny also contributes to podcasts in the disability space.

www.ingramcontent.com/pod-product-compliance
Lightning Source LLC
Chambersburg PA
CBHW072019290426
44109CB00018B/2287